Starting Sensory Integration Therapy

Fun Activities that Won't Destroy Your Home or Classroom!

by Bonnie Arnwine

Illustrated by Olivia McCoy

All marketing and publishing rights guaranteed to and reserved by

721 W. Abram Street
Arlington, Texas 76013
800-489-0727
817-277-0727
817-277-2270 (fax)

E-mail: info@FHautism.com
www.FHautism.com

Cover design: RedHare Studio, Saginaw, TX

Author's photo: Rachelle H. Freeman

Printed in the United States of America.

ISBN-13: 978-1-932565-47-8
ISBN-10: 1-932565-47-7

Dedication

To my husband, Geoffrey Arnwine, who encouraged me to write this book because he believed it would help other parents.

Acknowledgments

In a way, one could say this book has been in development for centuries. It is a collection of activities that caregivers have passed down for many years. I would like to begin by acknowledging this creative and collective spirit. By freely sharing their successes, past educators continue to shape and develop our children. For my part, this book has been a work in progress for the last nine years. It began when I started playing with my son.

Many people had a role in this book's development. I would like to start by thanking the staff at First Presbyterian Church Preschool. You helped me find services for my son, gave me a great job, shared with me many of the fun activities within this book, and encouraged me when times were tough. I love you!

Lori J. Davids, OTR, and Joan Reuveni for introducing me to the world of Sensory Processing Disorder and patiently teaching me how to help my son. You are both excellent practitioners and advocates. Your work improved the quality of my family's life forever. Words cannot express my thankfulness.

The children I have worked with in preschool and Sunday school for the last ten years. I have enjoyed working with each one of you. I would not have been able to try out my many experiments without you!

Finally, I want to acknowledge my two children—Geoffrey and Gracie. I would never have written this book without them. They have opened up a new world for me and I am a better person because of them.

Contents

Preface

Chances are, if you're reading this book, it's because you have a child or work with a child who has sensory integration dysfunction, also known as sensory processing disorder (SPD). This book is not filled with in-depth explanations or checklists designed to evaluate sensory processing disorder. What you will find are lots of fun, inexpensive, sensory activities that can be set up and cleaned up quickly in your home or facility. Each chapter contains activities based on a specific sensory need, and all activities require only common household items. "Extend It!" ideas are included to prolong a child's interest in the activity. After all, there is nothing worse than setting up a project that only holds a child's attention for two or three minutes! My son and I spent countless hours enjoying the activities in this book; I hope you and the children you care for will enjoy them also.

Bonnie Arnwine
January 2006

The Terms We Use to Describe Sensory Processing Disorder

In 2004, a committee of Occupational Therapists clarified the terms we use to describe sensory problems. The committee included Lucy Jane Miller, PhD, OTR, FAOTA; Sharon A. Cermak, EdD, OTR/L, FAOTA; Shelly J. Lane, PhD, OTR/L, FAOTA; and Marie E. Anzalone, ScD, OTR, FAOTA; as well as Beth Osten, OTR; and Stanley I. Greenspan, MD.

This chart,[1] which shows the various types of sensory processing problems, illustrates the many ways that sensory processing disorder can manifest itself in children. These types of sensory processing disorder can occur in any combination, resulting in a very large range of symptoms.

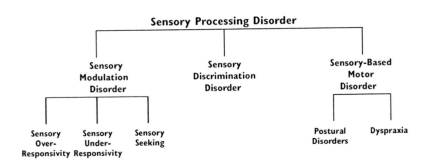

___

1 Chart reprinted from *The Goodenoughs Get in Sync* by Carol S. Kranowitz, published by Sensory Resources, 2004. Used with permission.

Chapter 1:
Our Senses

In order to understand sensory dysfunction, we need to understand the purpose of our senses. Our senses allow us to experience and respond to our environment. To experience a sunset, we look at it; when we feel cold we put on a jacket; if we smell smoke, we respond by getting out of the building. When our senses are working together properly, they protect us and allow us to enjoy our surroundings. The five senses most of us are familiar with are

Vision—visual perception

Hearing—auditory perception

Touch—tactile perception

Smell—olfactory perception

Taste—oral perception

Two senses we may not be familiar with are

Vestibular—Sensory information we receive from our middle ear that is related to movement and balance. As a child did you ever spin yourself in circles and then try to walk straight? You couldn't walk straight because your body was receiving impaired vestibular information.

Proprioceptive—Sensory information we receive from our muscles, joints, and body parts. Close your eyes and raise your hand in the air. You know where your hand is even though you are not looking at it because the muscles and joints in your hand and arm are sending information to your brain telling it the position of your hand.

These seven senses work together to help us understand and maneuver within our environment. For example to open a door,

1. We look at it. (visual perception)

2. We place our hand on the doorknob. (visual and tactile perception)

3. We squeeze the doorknob with the proper pressure and turn it. (tactile and proprioceptive perception)

4. We pull open the door with the right strength. (vestibular, proprioceptive, visual, and tactile perception) If the door has a squeaky hinge, we hear that as we are opening it. (auditory perception)

5. We walk through the doorway, stepping over the door-jamb. (visual, vestibular, and proprioceptive perception)

If our brains receive inaccurate sensory information, we may

- Bump into the door

- Slam the door

- Get hit with the door

- Trip or bang into the doorway as we walk through

- Be unable to open the door

What is Sensory Processing Disorder?

Sensory processing disorder (SPD) causes individual's bodies to misinterpret the sensory information received from the environment. One or more of their senses may over- or un-derreact to sensory information. Because their senses are not working together properly, people with SPD have difficulty re-sponding effectively to their environment.

The Overreactive or Hyper-reactive Response

People who are overreactive to sensory stimulation may re-spond to certain harmless sensations as if they are dangerous or painful.

They may

- Avoid letting people touch them

- Become agitated if a peer accidentally bumps them

- Scream during hair washing or brushing

- Gag on or avoid certain textures of food
- Scream or cover their ears if they hear a vacuum cleaner or dog barking
- Fear ordinary movement activities like swings, slides, or ramps

The Underreactive or Hypo-reactive Response

People who are underreactive to sensory information need higher levels of stimulation in order to respond to their environment. They may seek intense stimulation or shy away from sensory stimulation.

They may

- Seem immune to pain, not noticing cuts, bruises, or other injuries
- Chew on inedible objects, such as their clothing, toys, or objects they find on the ground (e.g., woodchips, sand, or sticks)
- Bump or crash into things
- Tire easily
- Avoid contact with others

A Combination of Responses

Some people may be hyper-reactive to certain sensory information and hypo-reactive to other types of sensory information. For example, a child could be hypo-reactive to touch (tactile information), constantly chewing clothing and seeking things to smear. At the same time, this child may be hyper-reactive to noise (auditory information), covering her ears and screaming every time the vacuum cleaner is turned on.

SPD is a complex condition. To accurately assess SPD, a knowledgeable professional must complete a series of assessments. This person is usually an occupational therapist (OT). Once a child is assessed, symptoms and behaviors related to SPD will be defined and a sensory diet may be prescribed to address the dysfunction.

A Sensory Diet

A sensory diet is simply a variety of sensory experiences designed to help a child with SPD properly interpret his or her environment. For example, if a person is diagnosed with heart disease, a doctor will prescribe a healthy cardiovascular diet—one low in fat that contains lots of fruits and vegetables—and an exercise program. Similarly, an OT may prescribe a healthy sensory diet. It may be rich in tactile experiences, such as a brushing program, as well as certain physical games designed to enhance vestibular stimulation.

Speaking of diets, have you ever failed at a diet? Many times people fail at changing their diet because the diet does not satisfy their needs. They want to stick with it, but they are unable to because they felt hungry or deprived of something they crave.

Hypo-reactive children may feel the same way—hungry for certain types of sensory stimulation. Exasperated, a parent of a child who is hypo-reactive to touch may tell his child to stop smearing the toothpaste. The child may want to stop, knowing that this activity is unacceptable behavior; however, the craving for sensory input drives her to continue smearing the toothpaste. In cases like this, it is our job to feed a child's sensory needs in an appropriate manner, not restrict it.

Conversely, hyper-reactive children may restrict certain types of sensory stimulation to the extent that they become "malnourished." In this case, we must make sure hyper-reactive children get a balanced diet of sensory experiences that they also enjoy.

Starting Sensory Integration Therapy

A close working relationship with a child's therapist is essential to administering an effective program. The therapist will have good ideas and strategies for adapting activities or challenging the child appropriately and be aware of behaviors and signals to watch for. The therapist can evaluate progress and give suggestions to keep the child progressing. **Always consult a child's therapist before trying new activities or whenever questions arise**. Please remember that not all of the activities in this book are appropriate for every child.

Follow Your Child's Lead!

Children frequently come up with innovative and fun extensions of activities. When they are allowed to explore new ideas, create new scenarios, and take on new roles, they stay active and interested in the activity. As long as the play is safe—and it doesn't enhance or encourage unhealthy behaviors—anything goes!

Life Is a Series of Small Steps.

I have many dear friends that began sensory integration therapy with their children at the time I began working with my son. Our children are more confident, relaxed, and less fearful, better at interpreting their environment today than when we first started therapy. Sensory integration therapy also provided lots of positive interaction with our children along the way! I hope these activities will be fun and helpful to you as well. Best wishes on your journey ahead.

Chapter 2:
Tactile—Touch Activities

The house was too quiet. I called out for my son, but only heard wild laughter. I followed the laughter down the hall to the living room, turned a corner, and almost passed out. My son was lying on the coffee table swimming in maple syrup! He looked at me, smiled, and did the breaststroke. I watched in horror as tiny drops of maple syrup dripped off the table onto the carpet. The next couple of hours were a blur of showering, scrubbing, and carpet cleaning. I felt like putting locks on my refrigerator and cabinets!

Later that week, I met with my son's occupational therapist. I shared my syrup experience and my frustration. She explained that my son was not disobedient or out of control; his body was directing him to what he needed—lots of tactile stimulation! Once I started providing lots of tactile activities, my messy surprises started to disappear. This chapter contains many of our favorites.

Shaving Cream Fun

A tip for easy cleanup—do these activities in the bathtub. Shaving cream is water-soluble and will wash right off. You may want to use an unscented type for sensitive skin since some children react to strong smells. Try this activity in the evening before bath time. You can also enjoy this activity at a table with a cookie sheet. I keep a special activity towel nearby for all of our messy fun. If you are doing this activity in the classroom, use masking tape to section off areas of the table for each student. this is a great activity if your table is stained or has dried paint on it, as the shaving cream cleans the table nicely.

What You Will Need

Plain shaving cream

Food coloring

Small plastic containers

Large cookie sheet

Towel

Optional Items

Toy cars, dinosaurs, or other plastic animals

Sponges, Q-tips®, paintbrushes, cotton balls

Begin by spreading a baseball-size amount of shaving cream on the side of the bathtub or on a cookie sheet. Allow the child to finger paint with the shaving cream.

You may suggest toe-painting as well. **Caution:** *This can be very slippery!* Make sure the child is sitting down and her body has plenty of support, so she doesn't fall. You may want to support her by holding her under the arms. Allow her to lean back and paint with her feet. You can also easily toe-paint outside. Place a cookie sheet with shaving cream on some grass. Have the child sit next to it, either on the grass or in a chair for support, as she paints with her toes. When it's time to clean up, rinse off her feet with a hose and dry with your activity towel.

Extend It!

Color Mixing

Fill two small plastic containers each with baseball-size amounts of shaving cream. Add two drops of food coloring to each container and mix up. Primary colors (red, yellow, and blue) work best. Place the colors next to each other and encourage the child to mix them and make a new color.

Shaving Cream Paints

Fill a couple of small plastic containers with baseball-size amounts of shaving cream. Add two drops of food coloring to each container and mix up. The child can finger paint with the colors or paint with paintbrushes, Q-tips,® cotton balls, or sponges.

Making Tracks

Plastic dinosaurs, toy animals, action figures, or toy cars can make tracks through the shaving cream.

Rubbing

Be sure to spread some newspaper or garbage bags down on the table before starting this activity, especially if your crayons are not washable. To make this activity even easier, use washable crayons.

What You Will Need

Crayons

Chalk

Inexpensive paper

Empty cereal boxes

Optional Items

Coins, embossed cards, silverware handles, leaves, other textured items

Take an empty cereal box and cut it into various small shapes. Place them under a sheet of paper, and let the child rub chalk or color on the paper with crayons until he sees the imprints of the shapes. You can also use other flat objects such as coins, embossed cards, silverware handles, etc. instead of the cardboard shapes.

Extend It!

Nature Walk

Go outside with paper and chalk. Let the child find things to use for rubbing, such as leaves, flowers, small twigs, tire tread, or tree bark. There are so many interesting things to touch and feel outdoors—the sky is the limit!

Paper Leaves

Gather several leaves from outside. Place them under a sheet of paper and encourage the child to color the paper with a crayon to make the imprints show through. Cut out the colored leaves.

"Squishies"

These simple, homemade "squishies" can be very calming and last quite a long time. If your child is aggressive with her squeezing, use two balloons.

What You Will Need

Sand, salt, rice, birdseed, or flour

Funnel (or a paper plate folded into a funnel shape)

Balloons (medium-sized)

Pencil or small spoon

Optional Items

Tempura paint (or other "kid" paint), dish detergent, shallow bowl, paper bag or butcher paper

Using a funnel, fill each balloon with a cup of one or two grainy ingredients. If you are having trouble filling the balloons, use a pencil or small spoon to gently push the material in. Tie the balloons shut, making sure you have squeezed out any extra air. Give it to your child and let her squeeze away!

Extend It!

Squishy Painting

Mix one to two tablespoons of tempura paint with a squirt of dish detergent in a shallow bowl. This will keep the paint from splattering and make cleanup much easier. If you don't have tempura paint, almost any kind of "kid paint" will work; I've even used shaving cream paint. Use the paint to make wrapping paper by dipping the squishy into the paint and stamping a paper bag or a sheet of butcher paper.

Squishy Box

Make several types of squishies. Fill different balloons with sand, flour, salt, rice, beans, birdseed, and so on. Put the squishies in a shoebox, and you have your own squishy box— a variety for the child to choose from!

Pass the Squishy

This game was inspired by the old game Hot Potato. Sing the song below to the tune of "London Bridge." Use the speed of your singing to control the speed of the game. As the song is sung slowly, pass the squishy slowly. As you speed up your singing, the pace of the game should also increase.

> *Pass the squishy, pass it now, pass it now, pass it now.*

> *Pass the squishy, pass it now, pass it now.*

Variations

> *Pass it fast*

> *Pass it slow*

> *Pass it high*

> *Pass it low*

Shampoo Finger Paints

Do this in the bathtub for easy cleanup. It's perfect in the evening before bath time. You can also do this on a large cookie sheet or on the shiny side of freezer paper. The butcher has always been kind enough to give me extra paper when I ask him.

What You Will Need

    White or colorless shampoo

    Food coloring

    Small plastic cups or muffin tins

    Large cookie sheet or freezer paper

    Towel

Optional Items

    Salt or sawdust

    Cotton balls, Q-tips®, sponges, paintbrushes, combs, or
        Popsicle® sticks

    Toy cars, dinosaurs, or other small plastic animals

Pour small amounts of shampoo, each about the size of a quarter, into cups. Add two drops of food coloring, different colors in each cup, and blend together. Make two or three colors. Allow the child to finger paint on the cookie sheet, freezer paper, or bathtub walls. For texture, add salt or sawdust to the finger paint. (If you're using sawdust, don't do this activity in the bathtub!)

Extend It!

More Painting Fun

Encourage the child to paint with paintbrushes, combs, Popsicle sticks, Q-tips, cotton balls or sponges.

Sponge Prints

Cut a few sponges into simple shapes. Allow the child to make prints with the paint.

Lather up

Give the child wet sponges. Let him rub the paint back and forth to make thick foamy lather. Once it's lathered up, he can finger paint in it some more. For more fun, add some toy cars, dinosaurs or animals and let him make tracks in the lather.

This activity also can be done with gel, apricot facial scrub, or cold cream. For a child hyperreactive to smells, use unscented products.

Hair Gel Bags

This squishy bag is very easy to create, and will last quite awhile (if it is not bitten!) If your child is particularly aggressive use two bags.

What You Will Need

> Hair gel
>
> Sparkly items
>
> Ziploc® sandwich bags
>
> Duct tape

Optional Items

> Grocery bag or large sheet of paper
>
> Beads

Open a Ziploc bag and squirt about a ¼ cup of hair gel inside. Place a few sparkly items, such as glitter or sequins, inside the bag as well. Close the bag securely, seal it with duct tape at the zipper end, and let the child squish the contents around.

Extend It!

Tic-Tac-Toe

Make ten hair gel bags, five each of two colors. Draw a large Tic-Tac-Toe grid on a piece of paper or grocery bag and play Tic-Tac-Toe. Instead of Xs and Os, one person uses hair gel bags of one color, and the other participant uses the second color. Add beads to the bags for more texture.

Tracing Fun

Place a simple maze or design under the hair gel bag. Have the child trace her way through the maze or trace the design through the bag.

Edible Finger Paint

For easy cleanup, place some newspaper on the table. Allow the child to finger paint on a clean cookie sheet instead of using paper.

What You Will Need

Prepared vanilla pudding or plain yogurt

Food coloring

Muffin tin

Cookie sheet

Newspaper

Put a large spoonful of pudding or yogurt into each muffin tin. Add one or two drops of food coloring to each tin and mix well. Allow the child to finger paint on a cookie sheet. These paints dry shiny and with texture. After the child is done, he can eat what's left or lick the picture he made!

Spaghetti Fun

These activities are very silly.

What You Will Need

Cooked spaghetti

Small balls

Finger paint or other
"kid paint"

Pie tins

Paper or large cookie sheet

Large pot of water

Spaghetti Painting

Cook some spaghetti with oil in the water to keep it from sticking. Have the child dip the spaghetti into pie tins of paint. Let her paint with the spaghetti on paper or a large cookie sheet. If using her hands is too challenging at first, suggest using tongs.

Spaghetti & Meatballs

Cook some spaghetti and put it in a large pot of cool water. Add some small rubber balls to the pot. Place the pot in the kitchen sink and let the child play with the spaghetti and meatballs. This activity is also nice to do during recess on the grass.

Spaghetti Writing

Cook some spaghetti with oil in the water to keep it from sticking. Trace letters, numbers, or the child's name on a piece of paper. Let him outline the letters with spaghetti.

Play Dough

There are several ways to keep the fun with less mess. If you have a small plastic swimming pool, let your child play with the play dough inside it. At the table, take a large cookie sheet, set a rubber mat under it so it will not slide, and let the child play with the play dough there. Spread an inexpensive vinyl tablecloth under the child's chair. When he is done playing, shake out and fold up the tablecloth, and throw away the play dough.

Caution: If play dough gets on your carpet, do not get it wet. This will make it much more difficult to clean. Let it dry, break it apart, and vacuum it up.

What You Will Need
Cooked Recipe
> 1 ½ cups flour
>
> ¾ cup salt
>
> 3 tablespoons cream of tartar
>
> 1 ½ cups of water
>
> 3 tablespoons oil
>
> Food coloring
>
> Medium bowl
>
> Large bowl
>
> 8" x 8" pan
>
> Resealable bags or containers

Mix together the dry ingredients in a medium-sized bowl. In a large bowl, combine the liquid ingredients, then stir in the mixed dry ingredients. Bake in an 8" x 8" pan at 350°F for seven to ten minutes. Cool and knead. Store in a resealable bag or yogurt cups to keep it fresh.

Uncooked Recipe

 2 cups flour

 1 cup salt

 1 cup warm water

 Food coloring

 Large bowl

 Resealable bags or containers

Optional Items

 Cookie cutters and plastic kitchen utensils

 Beans, beads, or rice

 Latex or vinyl glove[1]

In a large bowl, mix together the food coloring and water, then add the dry ingredients. Knead the dough until it is well blended. If your child is inclined, let her knead the dough. For something different, pour the ingredients in a resealable bag and close it tight, making sure to get all of the air out. Give the bag to the child and let her knead the ingredients until they are blended. Provide cookie cutters and plastic kitchen utensils and let her play. Store dough in resealable bags or containers.

Extend It!

Color Mixing

Take a ball of yellow and a ball of blue, and mix together to make green.

Bumpy Dough

Mix beans or beads in the play dough.

Squishy Gloves

Put play dough (or rice) into a latex glove. Tie the top and let your child squish!

---

1. Many people are allergic to latex. If allergies are a concern, use a vinyl or other non-latex glove.

Blubber

A child can play with blubber just like play dough. It has a bouncy, rubbery, stretchy feel. *Be careful: If this dries on carpet, it is very difficult to remove.*

At the table, set a large cookie sheet on a rubber mat, so it will not slide. Spread an inexpensive vinyl tablecloth under the child's chair. After the activity, fold the tablecloth and throw out the leftover blubber. Blubber can be stored in a sealed container for several weeks.

Caution! Don't put blubber or other goopy substances down the drain. They may clog it! Always throw blubber away in the trash.

What You Will Need

> 1 teaspoon 20 Mule Team® Borax natural laundry booster
>
> 1 cup water
>
> 4 ounces white glue
>
> 4 ounces water
>
> 7-10 drops of food coloring
>
> 2 bowls
>
> Plastic knives, cookie cutters, mini rolling pins

In one bowl, mix Borax with one cup of warm water until dissolved. In a second bowl, mix glue with four ounces of water and food coloring. Slowly pour the glue mixture into the Borax and water while stirring. Roll the blubber in the water mixture three or four times. Pull out the blubber and rinse it off in cold water. Provide plastic knives, cookie cutters, and mini rolling pins and let the child cut, flatten, and try to shape the blubber.

Add more or less water to the glue to change the consistency of the blubber. For this mixture, a little food coloring goes a long way. Too much coloring can transfer to the child's hands or the table.

Beans, Rice, and Birdseed Fun

This is a very messy activity. The trick to easier cleanup is to do it in the bathtub or in a small plastic swimming pool. Make sure the drain in the tub is plugged, and the tub or swimming pool is dry. When finished, just sweep up the beans and put them in a bin for reuse. Two-gallon stackable containers work well for storage.

What You Will Need

Beans, rice, birdseed, dry macaroni, or oatmeal

Large plastic bin or large pot

Sand toys

Optional Items

Cooking utensils, plastic cups, funnels

Small plastic animals or toy cars

Pour any combination of beans, rice, birdseed, or other dry grainy substances into a large plastic bin or pot (placed in the bathtub or plastic swim pool). Let the child play in it.

Extend It!

Cooking

Introduce cooking utensils, plastic cups, spoons, and funnels and encourage the child to pretend to cook. He can measure ingredients, stir them, add new ingredients, and so on.

Hide and Seek

Hide small plastic animals, cars, and trains and let the child find them.

Pud

Pud feels hard when grabbed, yet will turn into a liquid when you let go.

This is a messy activity. If the pud is colored with food coloring it will come off on the child's hands. However, if you have a child really craving tactile stimulation, it's great. Set the container on top of a cookie sheet, newspaper, or grocery bag for easy cleanup.

What You Will Need

> 1 cup cornstarch
>
> 1 cup water
>
> Food coloring

Optional Items

> Plastic dinosaurs or small plastic airplanes

Mix water and a couple of drops of food coloring together in a pot or two-quart container. ***Caution****: If your container is plastic, the food coloring may stain it!* Slowly add the cornstarch and wait a couple of minutes. Let your child play in the "pud."

Extend It!

Dinosaur Fun

Add black or brown food coloring (or mix various colors for this effect) to make a tar pit. Add small plastic dinosaurs and let them get stuck. Make tracks and watch them disappear. Have the child excavate the tar pit by digging up the dinosaurs.

Flying Fun

Color the pud blue. Add some small plastic airplanes and let the child fly them in and out of the pud.

Paint Dough

This paint is three dimensional and glossy when dry.

The paint stays contained, so this activity is not as messy. Simply cover the table with a vinyl tablecloth or newspaper.

What You Will Need

¼ cup flour

¼ cup salt

¼ cup water

Ziploc® bags or squeeze bottles

Food coloring

Paper or cookie sheet

Towel

Vinyl tablecloth
or newspaper

Optional Items

Muffin tin

Sponges, cotton balls,
paintbrushes

Cardboard

Beans, grains, or beads

Pour the dry ingredients into a Ziploc® bag. You can also use plastic squeeze bottles (such as empty ketchup or mustard bottles). Then mix together the water and food coloring and add them to the dry ingredients. Seal the baggie, making sure there is no air in the bag. Give the child the bag and let her squish it until the ingredients are mixed together, or let her shake the bottle until ingredients are combined. Cut a hole in the corner of the baggie and allow the child to squeeze out paint dough onto paper or a cookie sheet.

Extend It!

Paint

Fill muffin tins with several colors of paint dough. Allow the child to paint using sponges, cotton balls, paintbrushes, or his fingers.

Name Board

Write a child's name on a piece of cardboard. Encourage her to cover the letters with paint dough. Decorate the dough with beans, grains, or beads.

"No-Cook" Cooking

Fun, easy, and edible!

Peanut Butter Cookies

Make and eat in five minutes!

What You Will Need

1 tablespoon peanut butter

1 tablespoon nonfat milk

1 graham cracker

Resealable sandwich bags

Cake pan

Optional Items

Coconut or sprinkles

Place a graham cracker inside a cake pan, and have the child use his fingers to crumble it into fine pieces. Place the crumbs into a sandwich bag. Add the peanut butter and nonfat milk to the bag. Seal the bag, making sure all of the air is out. Have the child knead the bag until the ingredients are mixed. Open the bag, take out the dough, roll it into small balls, and eat. Roll the cookies in sprinkles or coconut for an added treat!

Ant Farm

What You Will Need

Graham crackers

Chocolate sprinkles

Resealable sandwich bags

Cake pan

Optional Items

Raisins or gummy worms

Place a graham cracker inside a cake pan, and have the child use her fingers to crumble it into fine pieces. Place the crumbs into a sandwich bag. Give the child a shaker with chocolate sprinkles and let her sprinkle in the ants. Close the bag and shake it up. Let the child eat the ant farm using her fingers or a small spoon. For variety, use raisins or gummy worms instead of sprinkles.

Watermelon Slushie

What You Will Need

Seedless watermelon

Resealable sandwich bag

Straw

Spoon

Plastic knife

Give the child a slice of melon (without the rind) and a plastic knife. Let the child cut the melon into small cubes and place them into the bag. Seal the bag, and have the child squish the melon to make juice. Afterward, open a corner of the bag and insert a straw. Let the child drink the juice. Give him a spoon to eat the leftover pulp.

Easy Doughnuts

What You Will Need

Electric skillet or shallow pan

Oil

Cookie sheet

Flour

Canned biscuits

Resealable sandwich bag

Cinnamon

Confectioners sugar

Optional Items

Cocoa powder

Heat the oil in an electric skillet. Cover a cookie sheet with a small amount of flour and place a biscuit on the flour coating. Put the cookie sheet on the table in front of the child. Allow the child to roll the dough into a long line. Then have her bring both ends together to make a doughnut. Cook the doughnut in the skillet until golden brown. **Be careful! Hot oil burns**! When it has cooled, give the child a baggie with confectioners sugar and cinnamon in it, and have her shake her donut in it to coat.

Extend It!

Fried Worms

Have the child roll the dough into a long line to make a worm. Cook the worm in the heated oil. When it has cooled, give the child a baggie with a scoop of cocoa in it, and let him cover the worm with dirt.

Hamburgers, Hot Dogs, & Condiments, too!

These activities feel great and can be very calming.

What You Will Need

Couch cushions

Blanket

Hamburger

Take a couch cushion and lay it on the floor. Have the child lie on the cushion, making sure her head is sticking out. Place another cushion on top of her. ***Caution****: Be sure the child's head is not between the cushions.* Kneel down by the child and slowly squish down on the top cushion applying pressure. Go slowly, and ask the child if she wants you to keep pushing or if you should stop.

Extend It!

While maintaining the pressure, extend the activity by moving the top cushion in circles to put on ketchup, rubbing back and forth to add mustard, or gently bouncing the top cushion to add pickles, lettuce, and tomatoes.

Hot Dog

Spread a blanket on the floor. Have the child lie down at the edge of the blanket with his head sticking out off the edge of the blanket. Roll the child up tightly in the blanket. *Caution: Be sure the child is comfortable, and the child's head is not in the blanket.* Ask if he would like some ketchup. If the child says yes, rub across his body to add ketchup. Ask if the child would like relish, mustard, peanut butter, or whatever you both can think of. Change the way you rub his body for each condiment.

Condiments

This time you become the hamburger or the hot dog. Ask the child for some ketchup. Have her extend her arm, grasp firmly at the top of the arm, and squeeze down pretending her arm is the ketchup bottle. Ask for mustard, and have the child use the other arm. Use a leg for mayonnaise, and so on.

Bird Feeder

To cut down on the mess, use only a quarter inch of birdseed in a small cake pan and use a **large** cookie sheet.

What You Will Need

Toilet paper roll or pinecone

Peanut butter

Birdseed

Yarn or string

Butter knife

Towel

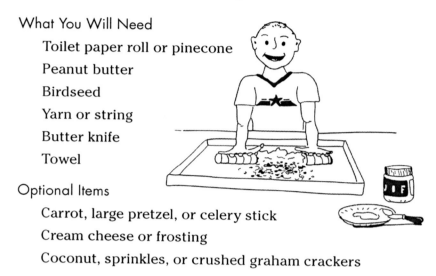

Optional Items

Carrot, large pretzel, or celery stick

Cream cheese or frosting

Coconut, sprinkles, or crushed graham crackers

Place a toilet paper roll or pinecone, a butter knife, and a small scoop of peanut butter on a paper plate. Set the paper plate on a cookie sheet at the table. Have the child cover the toilet paper roll or pinecone with peanut butter then roll it in birdseed. To hang the birdfeeder, punch a hole at one end, and tie a loop of string or yarn through the hole to make a hanger.

Extend It!

My Feeder

Give the child a carrot, large pretzel, or stick of celery to cover in peanut butter, cream cheese, or frosting. Let him roll it in coconut, sprinkles, or crushed graham crackers. Then let him eat it!

More Fun Feely Stuff

String Designs

When dry, this simple activity can be very pretty hung from string or taped to a window.

Use a wide, shallow bowl for the watered-down glue. Use a cookie sheet lined with aluminum foil or wax paper as a work surface. Also have a towel handy.

What You Will Need
    Yarn
    ¼ cup white glue
    ¼ cup water
    Wax paper or aluminum foil
    Cookie sheet
    Wide, shallow bowl
    Towel

Optional Items
    Clothespin
    Marker
    Paper
    Balloon, medium-sized

Mix the water and glue in a bowl. Cut several pieces of yarn, six– to twelve–inches long. Have the child dip the yarn in glue, then run her fingers down the yarn to squeeze off the excess. Encourage the child to make designs by placing the string on wax paper or aluminum foil. If touching the yarn is too challenging at first, allow the child to use a clothespin to dip and place the yarn.

Extend It!

Learn Your Letters

With a marker, write letters, numbers, or the child's name on a piece of paper. Ask the child to trace the design with the yarn.

Ornaments

Use holiday yarn. Draw a 6" x 6" box on the wax paper. Have the child make overlapping shapes with the yarn inside the box. Let the yarn dry, peel the design off the paper, and loop some more yarn through the top of the design to hang it for the holidays!

Bird in a Cage

Blow up a medium-sized balloon and tie it shut. Wet the yarn with the glue mixture and wrap it around the balloon until it resembles a cage. Let the yarn dry, pop the balloon, and pull out the pieces. Cut out a paper bird and punch a small hole in the top of it using a pencil. Hang the bird inside the cage with string. You can hang the cage in a child's bedroom as a pretend "pet," or liven up the windows of the classroom with colorful birds and cages. For this to work well, use a mixture of 2/3 cup glue and 1/3 cup water.

Eggshell Pictures

Remember to use a large cookie sheet for easy cleanup. To keep the glue from getting messy, make a glue tub. Cut a ½-inch hole in the top of a small plastic margarine tub. Fill the tub with ½ an inch of glue and put on the lid. Give the child a small paintbrush, and allow him to apply the glue with the brush. This is a great activity to do right after Easter.

What You Will Need

Heavy paper or cardboard

Newspaper

White glue

Small paintbrush

Food coloring

Vinegar

Hot water

Cups

Cracked eggshells

Large cookie sheet

Margarine tub or other disposable plastic bowl with lid

To Dye Eggshells

Combine half a cup of hot water, one teaspoon of vinegar, and 20 drops of food coloring. Make two or three colors following this procedure. Place the eggshells in the colors and let them soak for about five minutes. Take the eggshells out and place them on newspaper. Let them dry for about 10 minutes. When the eggshells are dry, crumble them into more pieces.

Draw an oval on some cardboard and paint it with glue. Have the child decorate the "egg" with shells.

Extend It!

Fun Pictures

Decorate simple pictures like butterflies, circles for planets, or flowers.

Soapy Fun

Filling a sink full of bubbles is a simple activity that's a lot of fun. An inexpensive hand-cranked eggbeater (bought at the store for five dollars!) was well worth the investment.

What You Will Need

Towel

Water

Dish detergent or bubble bath

Eggbeater, whisk, sponges, turkey baster, funnel, or plastic cups

Optional Items

Plastic baby doll

Handkerchiefs, socks, or potholders

Ice cubes

Plug the kitchen sink, pour in some soap, and add some water. Beat or whisk the water to create a fair amount of bubbles. Pour in the kitchen utensils and let the child have fun. Place a towel on the floor, so it won't get too slippery. If your child is really splashing a lot of water, put less in the sink, or do the activity in the bathtub.

To do this activity in the bathtub, place a large plastic bin filled with soapy water in the bathtub. Have the child sit next to the bin on a towel. ***Caution****: This can be very slippery.*

Extend It!

Wash the Baby

Give the child a washcloth and a plastic baby doll and let her wash the baby.

Laundry

Give the child several small items with different textures, such as handkerchiefs, socks, or potholders, and let him wash them, wring them out, and hang them to dry.

Arctic Fun

Instead of soap, put ice cubes in the water for some chilly fun. Freeze a large piece of ice to put in the water as an iceberg.

Tissue Paper Fun

Caution: *The ink from tissue paper can stain clothes or hands.*

What You Will Need

> White glue
>
> Water
>
> Paper cup or glue tub
>
> Tissue paper
>
> Construction paper
>
> Paintbrush
>
> Cookie sheet
>
> Newspaper

Optional Items

> Large plastic lid

Mix about two tablespoons of glue with one tablespoon of water in a paper cup or a glue tub. Cover a cookie sheet with newspaper. Place the glue and a piece of construction paper on the cookie sheet. Give the child several sheets of tissue paper to rip into pieces. Then have the child paint some glue onto the construction paper and press the tissue paper pieces on it to decorate it. She may want to crumple the paper or wad it into small balls, which is fine, too.

Extend It!

Sun Catcher

For this activity, you will also need a large plastic lid. Give the child a couple of different colored sheets of tissue and let him rip it into several pieces. Have the child paint the lid with glue. Then encourage him to decorate the lid with the torn tissue paper. Let the lid dry for a couple of days. When it is completely dry, peel the sun catcher out of the lid. Punch a hole in the top, and tie a ribbon through it. Hang it in the window. Remember to save the lid for another time. These look wonderful when hung in the classroom windows.

Crinkle Bag

What You Will Need

Old pillowcase, large garbage bag, or grocery bag

Fall leaves or crumpled newspaper

String

Fill an old pillowcase, large garbage bag, or plastic grocery bag with fallen leaves or newspaper and tie it shut. Let your child squeeze the bag, sit on it, or jump on it.

Bubble Wrap

Never throw bubble wrap away! Save it and let your child walk across it barefoot, rub it with her hands, or pop the bubbles.

Barefoot Fun

Take a barefoot walk. Walk on carpet and a tile floor, then go outside and walk on grass, cement, and finish by walking in some mud. Hose off your feet outside and dry them with your activity towel.

Chapter 3:
Gross Motor Activities
Vestibular & Proprioceptive

Most kids love tubes and slides. Many fast food restaurants have capitalized on this by making indoor playgrounds filled with this equipment. On a rainy Saturday, these play places are often filled to capacity with children having a great time. However, for some children this type of playground can seem like torture.

Tubes and slides—what's the big deal? They require accurate proprioceptive and vestibular information. For playgrounds to be fun, a child needs adequate balance and body awareness. If a child is not quite sure where her head is in relation to her surroundings, it's easy to bump it inside a tube. If a child's sense of balance is off, going down a slide can make her feel sick. Thus, for some children, tubes and slides are actually scary or even nauseating! To develop the vestibular and proprioceptive senses, children need a safe, stress-free environment to practice moving their bodies.

Fun With Boxes

Swimming Box

What You Will Need
Large box

Packing peanuts

Sand toys

Fill a large box half full with packing peanuts. Place the child inside the box with a plastic pail, shovel, measuring spoons, cups, and bowls. Let the child explore.

Smaller Version

What You Will Need
Small box or baby bathtub

Puffed cereal

Sand toys

Sheet or blanket

For a smaller swimming box, use a small cardboard box or plastic baby bathtub. Fill it with puffed wheat or rice cereal and some sand toys. For easy cleanup, place the box in the middle of a sheet or blanket on the floor. When the child is done playing, fold the blanket and dump the cereal or packing back into the cardboard box for use again later.

Extend It!

"Oh No, Where Did It Go?"

Put the large box in the middle of the room and let the child climb in. Say "Oh no, where did your head go?" Instruct the child to stick out his head. Repeat for hand, fingers, elbow, or leg. Have the child climb out of the box, lay it on its side, and call out body parts again.

Box Vehicles

Pretend a box is a vehicle. Have the child get in the box and give her a ride. Let her fill the box with her favorite toys to give them a ride.

Box Tunnels

Open two or more boxes on both ends and place them together to make a box tunnel. Encourage the child to crawl through it.

Movement Games

The following games are great for vestibular and proprioceptive input.

Beanbag Robot

Give the child a beanbag, and explain that he is a robot and the beanbag is his battery. Have the child move around like a robot, balancing the beanbag on his head. When the beanbag falls, tell him to freeze because a robot can't move without its battery. Change the position of the beanbag to the shoulder or outstretched hand and repeat the game.

Animal Game

Think up various types of animals with your child, then move like them.

> Snake—Slither on the ground.
>
> Rabbit or kangaroo—Jump up and down.
>
> Elephant—Clasp hands together and swing them back and forth.
>
> Cheetah—Run in place as fast as you can.
>
> Frog—Crouch down and jump up.
>
> Bird—Flap your arms.
>
> Penguin—Keep both arms down stiff at your sides and waddle.

Extend It!

Animal Charades

Make several cards, each with a different animal shown. Have the child choose a card and act out the animal while you try to guess what it is.

Animal Relays

Run like a bear on all fours. Move sideways on hands and knees like a crab. Squat low and hop like a bunny. Jump high like a kangaroo.

For variation, become different bugs: a worm, butterfly, bee, spider, or grasshopper.

Clapping Game

Lead your child in this game.

> *Clap your hands.*
>
> *Clap your hands fast, faster, fastest!*
>
> *Clap your hands slow, slower, slowest.*
>
> *Clap your hands high, high and fast, high and slow.*
>
> *Clap your hands low, low and fast, low and slow.*
>
> *Clap your hands big, bigger, biggest.*

You can also flap your arms, stomp your feet, or clap with your feet for variety.

Follow the Leader

Play follow the leader with the child. Jump up and down, walk backwards, shake your body, spin in circles, push on the wall, hop on one foot, and so on. Switch places and let the child be the leader.

Feather Game

What You Will Need

    Feathers

    Paper plate

Give the child a feather. Place a plate three feet away. See if she can throw the feather so that it hits the plate. Vary the distance a child stands from the plate.

Extend It!

Have the child switch arms, bend down, and look between his legs to throw, or turn around and throw it over his head.

Feather Relay

What You Will Need

    Couch cushions or cones

    Feather

    Paper plate

Place several couch cushions or cones around the room. Place a feather on a paper plate and hand it to the child. See if she can make her way around the cushions without letting the feather fall off of the plate.

Movement Songs

Recite or sing at a pace comfortable for the child.

Hammer Song

(To the tune of "Johnny Hammers with One Hammer")

I can work with one hammer, one hammer, one hammer.

The child is moving his arm up and down making a fist.

I can work with one hammer; I can work with two!

The child is moving both arms up and down making fists.

Continue the song in this pattern for these additional verses:

I can work with three!"

The child is moving both arms and stomping with one leg.

I can work with four!

The child is moving both arms and stomping with both legs.

I can work with five!

Now add the head nodding up and down.

Then work backwards:

*I can work with five hammers, five hammers,
    five hammers.*
I can work with five hammers, I can work with four!

"Head and Shoulders"

Have the child touch the body parts to correspond with the song lyrics.

Head and shoulders, knees and toes, knees and toes,
Head and shoulders, knees and toes, knees and toes,
Eyes and ears, a mouth and a nose,
Head and shoulders, knees and toes, knees and toes

"Little Red Wagon"

Bouncing up and down in my little red wagon,
Bouncing up and down in my little red wagon,
Bouncing up and down in my little red wagon,
Won't you be my darling!

Other verses:

Moving side to side in my little red wagon…"

Child sways left and right.

Now I'm rolling off of my little red wagon…"

Child rolls on the ground.

"Wheels on the Bus"

Child rolls her arms around each other.

> *The wheels on the bus go round and round,*
> *Round and round, round and round.*
> *The wheels on the bus go round and round,*
> *All through the town.*

Invent corresponding movements for each additional verse.

> *The doors on the bus go open and shut…*
> *The driver on the bus says, "Move on back!"…*
> *The people on the bus go bumpity-bump…*
> *The wipers on the bus go swish, swish, swish…*

"Mulberry Bush"

Child walks around an object representing a mulberry bush.

Here we go 'round the mulberry bush,

The mulberry bush, the mulberry bush.

Here we go 'round the mulberry bush,

So early in the morning!

Child pretends to dunk clothes into a bucket, scrub clothes on a washboard, and wring them out.

This is the way we wash our clothes,

Wash our clothes, wash our clothes.

This is the way we wash our clothes,

So early in the morning!

Other verses:

Child pretends to do the chore the verse describes.

This is the way we iron our clothes...

This is the way we scrub the floor...

This is the way we sweep the house...

Moving to Music

Bounce to the Music

Place the child on your lap. Sing a song with a definite beat, and bounce the child on your knees. Vary the tempos and beats. ***Caution:*** *Do not bounce too hard, and do not use this activity with very young children.*

Mirror Dance

Slow music works great for this activity. Put on some music and stand facing the child. Have the child copy your movements. Start with a simple movement like waving one hand above your head, then wave both hands, and so on. Switch roles, and let the child make up moves to be mirrored.

Freeze Dance

Play some music and have the child dance. When the music stops, he must freeze (stand still) until the music starts again.

Musical Hugs

Play some music and dance with your child. When the music stops, give each other a big hug.

Drum Your Body

Encourage the child to drum her body to the music. She can start by gently drumming on her head with her hands. Then move down the body drumming shoulders, chest, stomach, thighs, and feet.

Paper Plate Dancing

Give the child a paper plate. Play different types of music, and have the child keep the beat by tapping the plate on his head, tummy, knee, and elbow.

Toilet Paper Dancing

Give the child a length of toilet paper. This is her "streamer." Have her dance to music with her streamer. Instruct her to try not to let the streamer touch the ground. A scarf or paper streamers from the party supply store will also work.

Balloon Fun

What You Will Need

Balloons

Sticks for stirring paint (available at home improvement and paint stores)

Paper plates

Balloon Tennis

Blow up a balloon. Tape wooden paint stirrers to a couple of sturdy paper plates to make rackets. Toss the balloon in the air and play balloon tennis by tapping the balloon back and forth.

Balloon Catch

Have the child throw the balloon up in the air and catch it on the plate.

Balloon Dancing

Have the child dance holding the balloon. Swing it side to side, up and down, or make circles with it to the music. Or throw the balloon in the air and dance while trying to keep it from touching the floor.

Balloon Jump

Hang a balloon from the ceiling or a tree branch. Let the child jump and hit the balloon with his hands or head. Vary the height of the balloon.

Punching Bag

This is very simple to set up and take down.

What You Will Need
    Plastic grocery bag

    Newspaper

    Rope or heavy string

Optional Items
    Rubber ball

    Fallen leaves

Have the child help you fill a plastic grocery bag with crumpled newspaper. Tie the plastic bag shut and hang it by stringing rope through the handles. Let the child punch away. For a different feel, try stuffing a bag with leaves, or put a big rubber ball inside.

Taffy

Kids love making their own candy. From start to finish, this will take about two hours. The taffy needs to be pulled for 10 to 15 minutes. However, I prepared the taffy ahead of time and let my kids pull it after it cooled. Doing it this way, the actual activity time with my children was only 10 to 15 minutes.

What You Will Need

2 cups sugar

1 cup light-colored corn syrup

1 cup water

1 1/2 teaspoons salt

2 tablespoons butter

2 teaspoons vanilla

Candy thermometer

Wax paper or plastic wrap

Mix all of the ingredients except the vanilla in a medium saucepan over medium-high heat. When it boils, reduce the heat to medium, add the vanilla, and insert a candy thermometer. Continue to let the candy boil at a moderate rate stirring occasionally. Try to keep the temperature at about 250°F. After about 40 minutes, pour the candy onto a buttered cookie sheet. Let the candy cool for about 20 minutes.

Have the child butter her hands. (I sprayed my kids hands with cooking spray.) Help her twist and pull the candy until it turns a creamy color and feels very stiff, usually about 15 minutes. With buttered scissors, snip pulled strands of taffy into bite-sized pieces. Wrap the pieces in squares of wax paper or plastic wrap.

Hot Lava

My brother and I played this when we were little. It's great for a rainy day.

What You Will Need

> Couch cushions
>
> Towels

Take all of the cushions off the sofa and chairs. Scatter them on the floor within jumping distance of each other. Place a few cushions farther apart and place towels folded with a narrow surface area (like a balance beam) between them, connecting the two cushions. Tell the child the floor is hot lava, the cushions are islands, and the towels are bridges. Let him jump from island to island and balance on the bridges avoiding the hot lava.

Extend It!

Watch Out for Sharks!

Pretend the cushions are islands, the towels are bridges, and the floor is shark infested water. Designate one cushion as the boat. Have the child rock herself on the boat, back and forth, trying not to fall in the water.

Newspaper Fun

Paper Bag Faces

This is a very clean activity if the child decorates the bag with markers.

What You Will Need
Small paper bag

Stapler

Markers

Newspaper

Optional Items
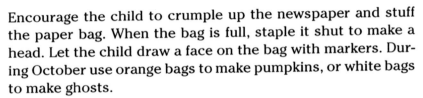
Yarn, sequins, buttons, felt, glue

Encourage the child to crumple up the newspaper and stuff the paper bag. When the bag is full, staple it shut to make a head. Let the child draw a face on the bag with markers. During October use orange bags to make pumpkins, or white bags to make ghosts.

For a more elaborate version, decorate the bags with yarn, sequins, buttons, and felt shapes.

Paper Race

Cut large pieces of newspaper into the shape of feet. Put one foot in front of you and one in front of the child. With another piece of folded newspaper, flap at the feet, moving it with the airflow. See who can "run" his or her foot to the other side of the room fastest. (Of course my son always won…)

Snowball Fight

Give the child a stack of newspapers. Have him crumple them up into several snowballs. When all of the paper is wadded up, have a snowball fight!

"Shake Something" Cooking

Ice Cream

There are two fun ways to make this great homemade treat. This is a clean activity, provided no one opens the bag! It takes five to seven minutes; to pass the time, sing some songs.

What You Will Need

> 1 cup whole milk
>
> 3 tablespoons sugar
>
> 1 teaspoon vanilla
>
> ¼ cup rock salt
>
> Ice (Crushed ice works best, but is not necessary.)
>
> 1 pint-sized resealable plastic bag
>
> 1 gallon-sized resealable plastic bag or 2 coffee cans with lids, one can larger than the other

Plastic Bag Method

Combine the milk, sugar, and vanilla. Pour the mixture into a pint-sized bag and seal. Fill a gallon-sized plastic bag half full of ice and pour in the rock salt. Place the smaller bag into the larger bag and seal the larger bag. Encourage the child to shake the bag for five to seven minutes. If the bag gets a hole and starts to leak, simply place it inside another resealable bag. When the ice cream is set, take the smaller bag out and snip off one of the corners. Let the child squeeze the ice cream into a bowl and eat it!

Coffee Can Method

Combine the milk, sugar, and vanilla in the smaller coffee can and put the lid on. Put the smaller can into the larger can. Fill the space between the two cans with ice and rock salt. Put the lid on the larger can. Roll the can back and forth between you and the child for five to seven minutes until the ice cream is set. If you have several children, you can sit in a circle and take turns rolling the can to each other.

Pudding

What You Will Need

Cold milk

Instant pudding mix

Empty yogurt cup and lid

Tape

Spoon

Fill a clean yogurt cup half full with cold milk and a teaspoon of instant pudding. Put the cover on the cup, tape it shut, and let the child shake it for a minute or two. Take the lid off the container and give her a spoon for an instant treat. You can also use baby food jars instead of yogurt cups.

Butter

What You Will Need

Heavy whipping cream

Empty yogurt cup and lid

Tape

Biscuit

Plastic knife

Honey

Fill a clean yogurt cup half full with whipping cream. Tape the lid shut. Shake for three to five minutes. Open the cup and scoop out the chunks of butter. For a different flavor, add some honey to the butter and spread it on a biscuit.

Making Sand

What You Will Need

Rocks

Coffee can with lid

Tape

This is a good nonedible alternative to "shake something" cooking. Fill a coffee can with several rocks and tape it shut. Roll the coffee can or shake it for several minutes. Open the can and see sand starting to form. For this to work best, use a softer type of rock. Using pieces of a broken brick works well.

Laundry Basket Fun

Give your child a laundry basket. Make a trail of canned food, shoes, or stuffed animals around the house. Have the child push the laundry basket around to collect the items. Have a prize waiting at the end of the trail.

Stocking Painting

To keep the paint from splattering too much, spread one large spoonful of paint into a pie tin or shallow container. You can also do this activity outdoors and use an old button-down shirt worn backwards as a smock.

What You Will Need

> Pantyhose
>
> Sand or kitty litter
>
> Paint (finger paint or other kid paint)
>
> Paper
>
> Shallow container

Spread some newspaper on a table. Fill the toe of the pantyhose with 1/4 cup of sand, and tie a knot to create a small ball. Leave about six inches of pantyhose above the knot and cut the rest off. Put a large spoonful of paint into a pie tin or shallow container. Let the child dip the ball in the paint then "bungee" the paint onto the paper. Holding the tail of the pantyhose, whack the ball part against the paper.

Rope Fun

These exercises are simple and easy to set up.

What You Will Need
    Piece of rope

Optional Items
    Ruler or other thin object such as a pencil
    Cardboard
    Beanbag

Snake

Tie one end of a piece of rope or a jump rope to a pole or table leg. Have the child make a snake by moving the rope back and forth. Tell her to make the snake slither fast, shaking the rope back and forth quickly. Have the snake move slowly. Tighten the slack on the rope to make skinny shakes. Give the rope more slack, so the child has to move her arms more back and forth to make big shakes.

Circles

Make circles with the rope. Sing the following to the tune of "London Bridge."

Make a circle, make it round, make it round, make it round.
Make a circle, make it round, make it round."

Variations
Make the circle big.
Make the circle small.
Make the circle fast (and sing the song quickly).
Make the circle slow (and sing the song slowly).

Pull it Down

Tie a piece of rope to a tree or pole and play tug-of-war. Can you pull down the pole?

Extend It!

Tug-of-War

Play tug-of-war with your child. Tie a piece of yarn or cloth to the middle of the rope as a marker, and place a ruler or other thin object on the ground between you. Whoever pulls the marker over the ruler wins.

Face Shake

Cut out a large cardboard circle with a hole in the middle. Draw two circles for the eyes, and draw a mouth. The hole in the center is the nose. Tie one end of a rope to a pole or table leg. Thread the other end of the rope through the hole in the face (the nose). Have the child hold the free end of the rope and start shaking the face. See how long it takes the face to move to the child.

Beanbag Jump

Tie a beanbag to the end of a piece of rope. Swing the bean-bag in a circle about three inches off the ground. Let the child jump over the beanbag as it approaches him. Switch places and have the child swing the beanbag in a circle while you jump over the rope.

Pull Me

You and the child both hold opposite ends of the rope. Take turns pulling each other around the house. Be careful not to pull your partner into anything!

Balance Beam

Lay a rope on the ground and use it as a balance beam.

Blanket Parachute

What You Will Need

    Blanket or sheet

    Teddy bear (or other stuffed animals)

Make Waves

Stand across from the child, each grasping opposite sides of the sheet or blanket. Shake the blanket to make waves.

Chariot

Have the child sit on one end of the blanket. Pick up the other side and give her a chariot ride, pulling her around on the blanket. Place stuffed animals and toys on the blanket and let the child give the toys a ride.

Bounce the Teddy

Place a Teddy bear on the blanket. Stand across from the child, each grasping opposite sides of the blanket. Both of you shake the blanket to bounce the Teddy.

Rock the Teddy

Place a Teddy bear on a blanket. Stand across from the child, each grasping opposite sides of the blanket. Both of you swing the blanket back and forth, rocking the Teddy on the blanket.

Spoon Relays

What You Will Need

Large spoon

Small potato

Cotton ball

Peanut

Place a bowl on one side of the room. Place a small potato, cotton ball, and peanut on the other side of the room. Give the child a spoon and have him walk to the potato, put it on the spoon, carry it to the bowl and drop it in. Have him repeat this for the cotton ball and the peanut.

Activities for Bilateral Motor Coordination

Bilateral motor coordination is the ability of both sides of the body to work well together. Initially children coordinate the left and right sides of their bodies symmetrically. Bringing both hands together to clap or catch a ball is an example of symmetrical coordination. Next, children learn to coordinate their bodies asymmetrically. Climbing steps, alternating left and right foot, is an example of asymmetrical coordination.

The following songs are great for bilateral motor coordination:

"Itsy Bitsy Spider"

"Wheels on the Bus"

"Johnny Hammers with One Hammer"

"Father Abraham"

"Hokey Pokey"

"Mexican Hat Dance"

"Chicken Dance"

Some other good activities are

Jumping jacks

Wheelbarrow walking

Martial arts

Gymnastics

Swimming

Yoga

Twister®

Activities for Crossing the Midline

Some children have difficulty with crossing the midline. If you were to draw an imaginary line down the center of their bodies, they would have difficulty moving their hands, feet, arms, or legs across that line to the other side of their body. Along with a variety of sensory issues, my friend's son Heath had difficulty crossing the midline. When Heath colored pictures, he used both hands. He passed crayons and markers back and forth, using his left hand to color the left side of the paper and his right hand for coloring the right side.

At first his mother thought this was wonderful; she thought he was ambidextrous. However, as school started problems with writing and reading began to emerge. School became so tedious for Heath that he often shut down and gave up.

I am happy to say Heath has shown a lot of improvement through consistent therapy, and he is now reading. My son also had difficulty crossing the midline. Keeping one of his hands occupied holding a squishy often made therapy much easier. We both really enjoyed the following activities.

Racing

This activity is easy to clean up if you place a plastic table cloth under the cookie sheet. When finished, fold the table cloth up, and dispose of the excess.

What You Will Need

> Cookie sheet
>
> Flour
>
> Toy cars

Optional Items

> Empty yogurt container with lid

Place a cookie sheet in front of the child. Sprinkle the cookie sheet with flour, so it barely covers the surface. Let the child make a racetrack with her finger in the flour. Make sure she does not switch hands, but crosses the midline. (You may want to give her a squishy to hold to keep one hand occupied.) Encourage her to make a large racetrack. Have her trace the outline of the track several times with her finger so that it is wide enough for the car. Once the racetrack is made, give her a small toy car to race on it. When the track becomes boring, smooth out the flour and make a new track.

Extend It!

Snow Day

Cut several holes in the lid of a clean empty yogurt container. Fill the container half full of flour. Let the child sprinkle "snow" all over the cookie sheet. Remember to only let him use one hand, so he is crossing the midline. Once it has finished snowing, have him use his finger to clear the snow off of the racetrack or street.

Secret Pictures

What You Will Need

    Watercolor paints

    Water

    Paintbrush

    White candle or white crayon

    White paper

    Cookie sheet

This is a fun classroom activity. Have kids make secret pictures for each other. Exchange the papers and let the kids reveal what their classmates drew. Using a white candle or crayon, draw a picture on a white piece of paper. Place the paper on a cookie sheet in front of the child. Have the child paint the paper with watercolors to find the secret picture. Make sure that the child does not switch hands, but paints back and forth across the midline.

Chapter 4:
Visual Activities

For Mimi, reading is torture. Along with a variety of sensory issues, she has ADHD. Her reading comprehension is poor because she must concentrate on tracking words so she doesn't lose her place in the text instead of concentrating on what she is reading. This tracking problem also leads her to frequently read the same sentence several times.

Although Mimi is a bright, fun-loving child, trying to get her homework done is a challenge every night for her and her family. Mimi receives both occupational and vision therapy and has improved significantly. Her parents are truly incredible! For kids like Mimi, sensory integration therapy as well as vision therapy may be warranted.

Homemade Tops

This simple activity fascinates young children the first time they watch it.

What You Will Need

Paper plate

Colored pens or crayons

Pencil

Have the child draw red, yellow, and blue dots on a plate. Push a pencil through the center of the plate. Spin the plate on the pencil, and rings of different colors appear.

Extend It!

Draw pictures or different shapes on a paper plate to see what will happen when you spin it.

Flashlight Fun

Planetarium

What You Will Need

Cereal box

Pencil

2 Flashlights

Construction paper (dark and bright colors)

Scissors

Punch several holes in an empty cereal box. Place a flashlight inside the cereal box and turn off the light. Turn on the flashlight and enjoy looking at the "stars" together. Turn the light back on.

Then take a piece of dark paper and cut out a simple shape of a rocket ship, small enough so it will fit the flashlight lens. Tape the outline on the lens of a second flashlight. Turn the light off. Turn on the first flashlight inside the cereal box. Give the child the other flashlight with the rocket outline taped to the lens. Turn the child's flashlight on and have him fly the rocket through the stars.

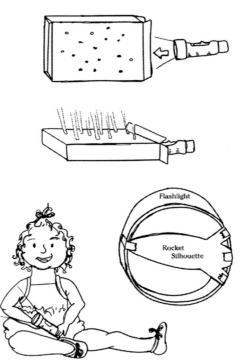

Flashlight

Rocket Silhouette

Rocket Tag

Use two pieces of dark paper to make two simple rocket ship shapes. Tape the rocket outlines to the lenses of two flashlights. Give a flashlight to your child, then turn off the light. Turn on both flashlights, and you and your child can play rocket tag. If your child likes trains or dinosaurs, you can play train tag or dinosaur tag—whatever is most interesting to him.

Space Exploration

Cut out several brightly colored circles for planets. Turn off the lights and let the child fly the rocket around a darkened room to find the planets.

Dropping Game

What You Will Need
> Plastic peanut butter jar, coffee can, or hat
>
> Clothespins, crayons, or other small objects

Have the child stand over a peanut butter jar, coffee can, or hat and try to drop clothespins, crayons, or other small objects in the container.

Extend It!

Place a coffee can, peanut butter jar, or hat on the ground. Have the child stand a few feet from it and try to throw small objects, such as pebbles, buttons, nuts, or dried beans, into it.

Tossing Games

Bean Bag Toss

What You Will Need

Beanbags or squishies

Cardboard box

Optional Items

Small, medium, and large boxes

Several large hats

Cut several holes of different sizes in the box. Encourage the child to toss beanbags through the holes.

Variation 1

Place a small, medium, and large box inside of each other. Assign ten points to the small box, five points to the medium box, and one point to the large box. Have the child throw beanbags into the boxes. See how many points a child can get with five throws.

Variation 2

Scatter several large hats on the floor. Encourage the child to stand about two feet from the hats and try to throw the beanbags into the hats.

Sink the Boat

What You Will Need

Water

Large plastic container

Small plastic container (such as a margarine cup)

Pennies or other small objects to toss

Fill the larger container with water. Place the smaller plastic container on top of the water, so it floats. Toss pennies into the boat until it sinks. You can also sink the boat with toy cars or pebbles.

Koosh® Catch

What You Will Need

Plastic milk jug

Koosh® ball

String

Scissors

Thoroughly clean a plastic milk jug and cut out the bottom. Tie one end of the string to the Koosh ball and the other end to the handle of the milk jug. Turn the jug over, throw the Koosh ball in the air, and try to catch it in the jug!

Block Bowling

What You Will Need

10 cardboard blocks or empty two-liter bottles

Ball

Set up the cardboard blocks or empty bottles in a triangular formation, the way bowling pins are set up. Give the child a ball and let her roll the ball at the "pins" to knock them down.

Block Relay

What You Will Need

Cardboard or wooden blocks

Have the child stand the blocks up on their smaller ends in a line like dominoes. Push over the first block and see if they will all fall down to make a block relay. Let the child experiment with different sized blocks, setting the distances farther apart.

I Spy

Sitting in a room, pick out an object (something obvious). Say, "I spy with my little eye something that is…" and describe the object until the child can pick out what you're describing.

Memory® I Spy

Place several cards from the Memory® game on the table with the pictures facing up. Say, "I spy with my little eye something that is…" and describe a card until the child chooses the card you are describing. The better she gets at the game, the more cards you can set on the table.

Helpful Games

Memory®

Guess Who®

Mazes

Dot-to-dot books

I Spy® books

Lite-Brite®

Chapter 5:
Hearing—Auditory Activities

My son was terrified of sound. Before I could vacuum, I had to warn him. He would run in his room, close the door, and cover his ears. When I finished, I would go into his room and find him with his head under the pillow.

He covered his ears at the sight of dogs or fire engines, fearing the noise they might make. While covering his ears protected his ears, it did not help him develop his auditory sense.

He needed exposure to sounds, and the only way we could do this, while ensuring he felt comfortable, was to initially let him control all of the sounds in our sound games. If I accidentally made my son uncomfortable, he would resist trying the activity again because it moved from being fun to scary. As you begin these activities with your child, remember slow and steady wins the race.

Making Music

Musical instruments are fun to make and play.

Shakers

What You Will Need

Any kind of container, such as plastic soda bottles or yogurt cups

Things to fill the containers, such as beads, rice, buttons, paper clips, sand, or birdseed

Construction paper

Tape

Markers

Place a handful of beads, beans, rice, or other filler into a container. Put the lid on the container and tape it shut. Decorate a piece of construction paper and tape it around the container.

Tambourine

What You Will Need

Aluminum (disposable) pie tins or paper plates

Things to fill the container, such as beads, rice, buttons, paper clips, sand, or birdseed

Stapler

Stickers or construction paper

Tape

Have the child fill one pie tin with a scoop of beads or other small items. Place another pie tin on top, creating a hollow space between the two containers, and staple its edges. Have the child decorate the tambourine with stickers or construction paper. Cover the staples with a small piece of tape.

Homemade Drum Set

What You Will Need

Several pots and pans

Wooden spoon

Place the pots and pans around the child. Give her a wooden spoon and let her pretend the pots are her drums and the wooden spoons the drumsticks.

What's That Sound?

What You Will Need

Small container with a lid such as a yogurt cup

Several small items, such as beans, rice, gravel, paper clips, and cotton balls

Optional Items

Household objects that make noise, such as a glass and spoon or broom

Musical instruments, such as a drum or whistle

Set several small items on a tray. Place several of one kind of item inside the container without showing your child. Shake the container, and ask him to guess which object is in the container.

Extend It!

Use any four items to make noise, such as a shaker cup with a small item in it, a glass and spoon, a broom, or a pot and wooden spoon. Have the child turn around with her back to you. Make a noise, such as sweeping the floor, and see if she can guess what it is.

Use four instruments to make noise, such as a tambourine, drum, whistle, and harmonica. Have the child turn around with his back to you. Make a noise, and see if he can guess the instrument.

Have the child turn her back to you. Clap three times and see if she can copy you without watching. You can also stomp your feet, bounce a ball, cough, hiccup, or shake a rattle.

Musical Drawing

What You Will Need

Music

Paper

Crayons

Give the child some paper and crayons. Instruct him to draw only while the music is playing. Try to vary the tempo of the music. Start and stop the music, and see if he can start and stop with it.

Sound Games

Sound Hide and Seek

For this game of hide and seek, use any kind of instrument that makes noise. The child hiding gets an instrument and makes noise until she is found. Some instrument ideas include a whistle, a harmonica, a bicycle horn, or a pot and a spoon.

Sound Hide and Seek #2

Have the child hide an object somewhere in the room. He must give you clapping clues as you try to find the object. The closer you come to the object, the louder the child should clap. The farther away you walk from the object, the softer the clap. Experiment with sounds; instead of clapping, the child can blow a whistle, play a harmonica, beat a pan with a wooden spoon, whatever seems fun and comfortable to him.

Marco Polo (Land Version)

Blindfold the child, and quietly position yourself somewhere in the room. Have the child call "Marco." Each time he calls, you reply with "Polo." You do not move during the game. This continues until the child finds you.

"When I Say Go" Obstacle Course

Set up a simple obstacle course. Describe to the child how to navigate the obstacle course. Have him touch the television, hop around a chair, take five steps backwards, walk across some couch cushions, or whatever seems fun. However, the child has to wait until you say, "Go." If he follows the directions before you say, "Go," he has to go back to the beginning of the course.

Treasure Hunt

Hide a small trinket somewhere in the house. Give the child clues to finding it. However, before she can follow the clues, she must wait until you say, "Go."

Chapter 6:
Smell

Josh loves to smell everything. While shopping at the grocery store, he picks up fruits, vegetables, meats, and boxed goods, smelling along the way. There was no such thing as a quick trip to the grocery store. What is a mother to do?

His mom's solution was to make an interesting smell necklace. He only wears it when they go grocery shopping. Since it hangs right around his neck, it keeps him occupied and allows his mother to get her shopping done. He doesn't tire of it quickly because he only gets to wear it on "special occasions."

How and where one provides therapy is only limited by one's imagination. If you would like to make a smell necklace with the child you are working with, check out the cinnamon rubbings on page 88. You can cut the sandpaper into various shapes, punch a hole in the shapes and hang it on some yarn for your own smell necklace fun.

Kool-Aid® Play Dough

I have found that most kids are tempted to taste this. They can try it—it is edible—but it tastes terrible. When I know several children will be playing with the play dough, I place a small amount in a separate container. Before the children start to play, I tell them there is play dough for tasting and play dough for playing, explaining that although it smells good, it tastes awful. Then I ask if anyone would like to taste it. I let them taste the clean play dough if they want to.

What You Will Need

   1 cup flour

   1 tablespoon vegetable oil

   1 package unsweetened Kool-Aid

   1/4 cup salt

   2 tablespoons cream of tartar

   1 cup water

Mix the dry ingredients in a medium pot. Add water and oil. Stir over medium heat for three to five minutes. When the mixture thickens and forms a ball in the pot, remove it, let it cool a bit, and knead until smooth. Seal in a plastic bag and refrigerate to cool more.

Cinnamon Dough

What You Will Need

1 cup ground cinnamon

1 ½ cups flour

2 cups hot water

Optional Items

Rolling pin

Cookie cutters

Pencil

String or yarn

Beads or beans

Wire hanger

Slowly add the cinnamon to the hot water. Then stir in the flour. Let the dough cool before kneading it. Use this dough just like any play dough.

Extend It!

Ornaments

Roll the dough flat using a rolling pin. Cut out shapes with a cookie cutter. Decorate the shapes with beans or beads. Use a pencil to poke a hole in the shape. Let dry for two to three days, then loop string through the hole for hanging.

Mobile

Create several ornaments. Using different lengths of yarn or string, tie them from a wire hanger to make a mobile.

Aroma Pictures

This art project smells great. Have the child work on a cookie sheet, and use a glue tub (see Eggshell Pictures on page 33) to keep the project less messy.

What You Will Need

> Coffee grounds
>
> Herbal tea
>
> Construction paper
>
> Glue
>
> Paper plates
>
> Cookie sheet

Draw a simple rectangle for a tree trunk and an oval for the top of the tree on some construction paper. Place a few tablespoons of coffee into a shallow bowl. Allow the child to paint the tree trunk with glue and decorate it by sprinkling the glue with coffee grounds. Pour the excess coffee back into the bowl. Tear open an herbal tea bag and place the contents in another shallow bowl. Have the child paint the glue on the oval then sprinkle the tea on for the leaves of the tree. Lay flat until dry.

You can also use potpourri to decorate the tree.

Extend It!

Draw simple animals like bears to decorate.

Use potpourri to decorate simple flower shapes.

Spicy Plates

To cut down on mess, use a glue tub (see Eggshell Pictures on page 33) and place everything the child will be working with inside a cookie sheet.

What You Will Need

Cinnamon

Cloves

Paprika

Pepper

Oregano

Curry

Paper plate

Pencil or marker

Glue

Cookie sheet

Draw lines to divide the paper plate into six sections. Have the child apply glue to each section and then sprinkle on a spice. Have the child tap off the extra spice into a bowl.

Cinnamon Rubbings

What You Will Need

Cinnamon sticks

Sandpaper

Encourage the child to draw a picture on the sandpaper with a cinnamon stick.

Extend It!

Necklace

After rubbing cinnamon on the sandpaper, cut the paper into several small shapes. Then punch a hole near the top of each sandpaper shape, and thread a piece of yarn through them. Tie a knot in the yarn to form a necklace that will fit over the child's head. She can smell the spicy sandpaper while wearing the necklace.

More Smells

For a variety of smells, you can also use ginger, dried citrus peels, or hickory chips.

Smelly Hide and Seek

What You Will Need

Several sandwich bags

Cotton balls

Cinnamon

Vinegar

Vanilla extract

Lemon juice or extract

In a baggie place one cotton ball scented with several drops of a strong smelling substance like lemon juice. Make a matching baggie. Create several smell sets with other scents. Hide one cotton ball of each smell around the room. Give the child a baggie with another scented cotton ball in it to see if he can find its smelly match hidden in the room. You can also use matching scented candles or potpourri packets.

Extend It!

Smell Hunt

Hide several baggies with different scents around the room and go on a smell hunt.

Toothbrush Fun

What You Will Need
>Toothbrush
>
>Toothpaste
>
>Cookie sheet
>
>Water

Optional Items
>Toys
>
>Toothpastes with different scents

Squirt some toothpaste onto a cookie sheet. Mix in a little water using the toothbrush. Let the child scrub the cookie sheet with the toothpaste.

Extend It!

Clean Something

Give the child some toys to clean with the toothbrush and some toothpaste.

Smell It

If your child has a strong need to smell, use different types of toothpaste, such as mint, bubble gum, or berry, and let her smell it as she scrubs.

Smelly Wood

Adding dish soap to this homemade paint makes it easier to clean up.

What You Will Need

Wood

Kool-Aid®

Paintbrush

Water

Cookie sheet

Optional Items

Sandpaper of differing grades

Kool-Aid stains easily. To set this project up, spread several sheets of newspaper on a table. Mix a package of Kool-Aid and a squirt of dish detergent with half a cup water to create the paint. Place the paint, a paintbrush, and a piece of wood on a cookie sheet in front of the child. Allow the child to paint the wood. The wood will smell for days.

Extend It!

Sand It

After the wood is dry, give the child some sandpaper and let him sand off the paint. It will release the Kool-Aid smell. For variety, use different grades of sand paper, one that is coarse and one that is very fine.

Smelly Paint

Coffee Paint

Add used coffee grounds to finger paint. Not only will children enjoy the smell; they may like the texture, too.

Kool-Aid® Paint

This paint smells great, but it will stain clothes. Add some sugar-free Kool-Aid powder to half a cup water. Add a squirt of dish soap to make it easier to clean up. Use this just like watercolors.

Smell Adventure

Walk around the neighborhood, and find different things to smell. Take in the scents of the trees, the grass, the flowers, and even the mud!

Walk around the house, and find different things to smell. Does one room smell better than another?

Smelly Bath

Fill a bathtub with water, and add scented bath salt, lemon peels, or cinnamon sticks for an aromatic bath.

Chapter 7:
Oral Motor

James has multiple developmental delays. At eight years old, he could not eat solid food. His diet consisted of yogurt, applesauce, and some baby food. Solid or slightly chunky food made him gag or throw up. He was often constipated and bloated. His diet was a serious health concern.

His family began oral motor exercises while slowly introducing more textured food to his diet. James now eats spaghetti noodles. It is a long slow road with some children, but many small steps lead to big accomplishments.

Bubble Fun

All Kinds of Bubbles

What You Will Need

Dish detergent

Water

20-ounce plastic bottles

Strawberry baskets

Wire hangers

Funnels

Pie tin

Fill a pie tin with water and some dish detergent. If you have a wire hanger, bend it into a diamond shape to make a giant bubble wand. Dip the diamond shape in the pie tin to get a soapy film over the opening. Encourage the child to gently blow at the film to make a big bubble.

To make a bubble horn, cut the bottom off of a 20-ounce plastic bottle. Dip the larger open end into the pie tin to get a soapy film over the opening. The child can blow through the smaller opening to make a big bubble appear. Let the child experiment with the different devices and create new ways to make bubbles.

Dancing with Bubbles

Turn on some music and blow some bubbles. Have the child try to keep the bubbles in the air by blowing them up while the music plays. ***Caution!*** *This can get slippery indoors!*

The child can also dance with feathers. While the music is playing, the child must keep the feather in the air by blowing on it.

Bubble Factory

This is good clean fun. You can do this outside, or inside sitting at a table. If at a table, place the bubble factory on a cookie sheet and have a towel near by for easy cleanup.

What You Will Need

Yogurt container with lid

Straw

Dish detergent

Water

Towel

Fill a clean yogurt container halfway with water. Squirt a tablespoon or two of dish liquid into the water and stir. Cut two small holes in the lid and place it on the container. Insert the straw in one hole. Let the child blow through the straw, and watch the bubbles pour out over the top of the cup and down the sides.

If you are worried that the child will suck the bubble solution up through the straw, poke a few small holes in the straw one inch from the top.

Bubble Wrapping Paper

Make homemade wrapping paper.

If bubbles get on a child's clothes, they may stain depending on how much food coloring is added to the bubble water. Have the child wear a smock or old shirt. For a quick and easy smock, use a plastic trash bag. Simply cut a hole in the bottom of the bag for the head and a hole on each side for the arms.

If you are worried the child will suck the bubble solution up the straw, poke a few small holes in the straw one inch from the top.

What You Will Need

Bowl

Straw

Dish detergent

Food coloring

Water

Paper

Fill a bowl halfway with water. Add two or three tablespoons of dish detergent and some food coloring. Place a straw in the bowl and have the child blow bubbles in the water. When a large amount of bubbles are on top of the water, place a sheet of paper on top of the bubbles. The bubbles will pop on the paper making a beautiful circular design. Then just let the paper dry.

Trees

To cut down on the mess, place the paper inside a cookie sheet before starting.

What You Will Need

    Paper

    Black or brown tempura paint (or other "kid" paint)

    Small dish

    Eyedropper

    Drinking straw

Optional Items

    Small container

    Water

    Dish detergent

    Food coloring

    Bubble wand

Fill an eyedropper with paint. Carefully drop a couple of spots of paint along the bottom of a piece of paper. Have the child blow at the paint through a drinking straw to make the tree trunk. Scatter some more paint above the trunk the child created, and have the child blow at it to make branches.

Extend It!

Fancy Tree

After blowing a tree trunk and branches, decorate the tree with bubble leaves. Fill a small container with water, dish detergent, and a few drops of food coloring. Give the child a bubble wand and let her blow bubbles onto the paper. The bubbles will pop on the tree branches making leaves!

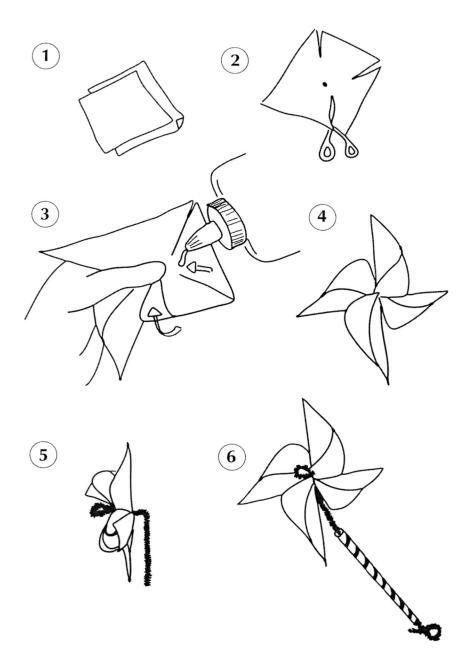

Pinwheels

What You Will Need

    Paper

    Glue stick or stapler

    Pencil

    Scissors

    Pipe cleaner

    Straw

    Crayons or bingo dotters

Cut out a five- to six-inch square of paper. From each corner of the square, make a straight cut towards the center of the square. Cut to within an inch of the center. Have the child decorate the pinwheel with crayons or bingo dotters. Paste down every other point (four out of eight points) to the center of the pinwheel. You can also staple the points.

With a pencil or the point of some scissors, poke a hole into the middle of the pinwheel. Run a pipe cleaner through the hole and make a little loop at the end of it in front of the pinwheel, so the pinwheel will stay on. Behind the pinwheel, bend the pipe cleaner at a right angle, leaving about a half inch between the back of the pinwheel and the bend, so the pinwheel can turn but will stay on the pipe cleaner. To give the handle of the pinwheel added strength, run the pipe cleaner handle through a straw. Make a loop in the pipe cleaner at the bottom of the straw, so the straw is secure.

Helpful Toys

Any kind of whistle

Blopens®

Harmonicas

Pinwheels

Kazoos

Recorders

Chapter 8:
Fine Motor Activities

Fine motor skills are precise muscle movements of the smaller muscles in your hands and toes. Frequently, children with sensory dysfunction also have poor fine motor skills. As with any muscle, it takes consistent steady exercise of these small muscles to improve performance. The more exercise these muscles get, the fitter they will become. The key to getting lots of fine motor exercise done with your child is to make it fun.

I did the following exercises with my son and the children I taught while I was a preschool teacher. They were usually a big hit with everyone.

Color Mixing

This fun activity is easy to clean up and set up if you make sure to place the ice cube tray inside a cookie sheet. However, food coloring may stain a child's clothes. Remember to roll up the child's sleeves or use a smock.

What You Will Need

Food coloring

Water

Eyedropper or medicine dropper

Ice cube tray or empty plastic egg carton

Cookie sheet

Optional Items

Large block of ice

Salt

Coffee filters

Paper towels

Fill three compartments of an ice cube tray or plastic egg carton with water. Put a couple of drops of food coloring in each compartment to make red, blue, and yellow water. Give the child an eyedropper and let him squeeze colors into the empty compartments and create new colors.

Extend It!

Freeze a large block of ice. Place it in the kitchen sink or in a large pot. Pour salt over the block and encourage the child to squeeze the watercolors onto the ice with the eyedropper.

Decorate coffee filters with colored water. Or cut paper towels into various shapes to be decorated. Remember to line a cookie sheet with newspaper for easy cleanup.

Popcorn Tree

For easy cleanup, use a large cookie sheet and a glue tub (see Eggshell Pictures on page 33).

What You Will Need

Paper

Popcorn (popped)

Popcorn kernels

Green food coloring

Paper towels

White glue

Optional Items

Brown marker

Other food coloring

Fill a bowl with one cup of water and green food coloring. Dip the popped corn in the green water for a couple of seconds, then let it dry on a paper towel.

On a piece of sturdy paper, draw a rectangle (for the trunk) with an oval on top (for the branches). Let the child paint the rectangle trunk area with glue and decorate it with popcorn kernels. Next, encourage the child to fill in the oval area with glue and decorate it with the green popcorn.

Extend It!

Spring Tree

With a brown marker, draw a tree and some branches on construction paper. Dye the popcorn pink or leave it white. Have the child glue blossoms on the branches.

My Name

Write the child's name on a piece of paper and allow her to trace her name with glue, then decorate with popcorn.

More Pictures

Color the popcorn different colors. Draw simple flowers, cars, trains, insects, or animals to decorate.

Marshmallow Sculptures

If you don't have small marshmallows, just cut larger marshmallows into quarters to make smaller pieces.

What You Will Need
Marshmallows, large and small

Toothpicks

Optional Items
Paper

Scissors

Raw veggies

Simple Spiders

Give the child one marshmallow. Encourage him to stick the marshmallow with eight toothpicks for legs.

Animals

Make animal sculptures. To make a lamb, give the child a large marshmallow for the body, several toothpicks for the legs and a neck, and smaller marshmallows for the head and feet.

Extend It!

Snowflakes

Cut a simple snowflake out of a piece of paper. Lay the snowflake flat on the table in front of the child. Encourage her to make a three-dimensional snowflake with the toothpicks and marshmallows using the paper snowflake as her guide.

Vegetable Sculptures

Provide several kinds of vegetables that can be eaten raw such as sliced cucumbers, carrots, celery, broccoli, and cauliflower. Encourage the child to use toothpicks to assemble vegetable sculptures.

What's in My Purse?

What You Will Need

Pairs of small common objects, such as crayons, keys, buttons, or baby socks

Purse

Put one of each item in the purse. Give the child an item and see if he can find the matching item inside the purse using only his sense of touch. No peeking!

Optional Items

2 paper bags, each containing the same objects

Coffee can containing three each of five different items

Extend It!

A New Version of "Go Fish"

Give two people a paper bag, each containing the same objects. The first player takes an object from her bag and asks the other player if he has the matching item. The second player reaches in his bag without looking, finds the match, and gives it to the other player. The second player takes a turn, asking for an object still in his bag. The first player gives him the item after she locates it using only her sense of touch. Continue until all the items are paired.

"Can You Find It?"

Place three each of five different items (e.g., three buttons, three paper clips, three clothespins, three cotton balls, and three quarters) inside a coffee can. Ask the child if she can find an item from each group without looking.

Bowl Relay

What You Will Need

Tweezers (tongs or clothespins can also be used.)

5 Bowls

Cotton balls

Popcorn

Small plastic animals

Dry macaroni

Optional Item

Music

Put a bowl with a few cotton balls in it on one side of the table. Place another bowl with some popcorn in it on another side of the table. On a third side of the table, place a bowl with small plastic animals in it. Place a bowl with dry macaroni in it on another side of the table. Give the child an empty bowl, and let him walk around the table, using the tweezers to place one of each item in his bowl. Make sure most of the items are easy at first. As the child improves his skill with the tweezers, add more difficult items to the relay.

Simpler Version

Put several cotton balls in a bowl and have the child use tongs to pick up the cotton balls and put them into another bowl. This can be a race if more than one child participates.

Extend It!

Musical Freeze Relay

Play some music while the child goes around the table, filling her bowl with items using tweezers. When the music stops, she has to freeze.

Musical Relay Race

Play some music as the child walks around the table with a bowl and, using the tweezers, fills it with as many items as he can. When the music stops, it is time for him to move to the next bowl. Continue this until the child has been to each bowl.

Cutting Fun

Practicing cutting is great to develop fine motor skills.

Some children may become frustrated by cutting because they close the scissors all the way and lose their place on the paper. To help with this, wrap tape around the inside of each handle so that the scissors don't close all the way.

What You Will Need

Comics from the newspaper

Postcards

Old birthday or holiday cards

Construction paper

Optional Items

Paper plates

Glue

Tape

Cutting Party

Place several different types of paper on the table and just let your child cut out whatever she can dream up.

Extend It!

Cut Collage

Have the child cut several strips of different types of paper. Glue them to a paper plate to make a collage.

Hula Skirt or Silly Wig

Draw a line four inches from the top of a piece of newspaper. Have the child cut long strips of fringe, from the bottom of the newspaper to the line, for a hula skirt. Once the cutting is done, use some tape to fasten it around the child's waist.

For variation, use the fringe as a silly wig. Place the paper on top of the child's head, and use tape to secure it snugly. Tape the wig at the uncut strip, fringe sticking up.

Helpful Toys and Games

Operation®

Battleship®

Ker-Plunk®

Yahtzee®

Cootie®

Hi Ho Cherry-O®

Lite-Brite®

Tinker Toys®

Duplos®

Legos®

Lincoln Logs®

Lacing Cards

Pegs & Peg Boards

Colorforms® or Stickers

Puzzles and Tangram Puzzles

Chinese Checkers

Index

chalk 10
cinnamon 27, 83, 85, 87, 88, 89, 92
clothespins 29, 70, 106, 107
cloves 87
cocoa powder 27
coconut 25, 30
coffee can 54, 56, 70, 106
coffee filters 102
coffee grounds 86, 92
coins 10
colors 8, 9, 13, 16, 18, 19, 20, 23, 33, 66, 68, 92, 102
combs 13
comics 109
construction paper 35, 69, 77, 86, 103, 109
cookie cutter 19, 20, 85
cornstarch 22
corn syrup 51
cotton balls 8, 9, 13, 23, 24, 79, 89, 106, 107, 108
crayon 10, 64, 66, 68, 70, 80, 99, 106
cream cheese 30
cream of tartar 18, 84
cups, plastic 13, 21, 34
curry 87
cushions 28, 42, 52, 81

D

detergent, dish 11, 34, 91, 94
dinosaurs 8, 9, 13, 14, 22, 70
doughnut 27
duct tape 15

E

eggshells 33
eyedropper 97, 102

F

feathers 42, 95
felt 53
finger paint 8, 9, 13, 14, 16, 17, 57, 92
flashlight 69, 70
flour 11, 12, 18, 19, 23, 27, 64, 65, 84, 85
food coloring 8, 9, 13, 16, 18, 19, 20, 22, 23, 33, 96, 97, 102, 103
freezer paper 13
frosting 30
funnel 11, 21, 34, 94

G

garbage bag 10, 36
glue 20, 31, 32, 33, 35, 53, 86, 99, 103, 109
graham crackers 26, 30
grains 23, 24

peanut butter 25, 29, 30
peanut 62
peanuts (packing) 38
pepper 87
pie tins 17, 77
pillowcase 36
pinecone 30
pipe cleaner 99
play dough 18, 19, 20, 84, 85
popcorn 103, 104, 107
popsicle sticks 13
postcards 109
potato 62
potpourri 86, 89
pretzel 30
proprioceptive 1, 2, 37
pud 22
pudding 16, 55
purse 106

Q

Q-tips 8, 9, 13

R

raisins 26
rice 11, 12, 19, 21, 38, 77, 79
rocks 56
rolling pin 20, 85
rope 50, 58, 59, 60
rubbings 83, 88

S

salt 11, 12, 13, 18, 19, 23, 51, 54, 84, 102
salt, rock 54
sand 11, 56, 57, 77
sandpaper 83, 88, 91
sand toys 21, 38
sandwich bag 15, 25, 26, 27, 89
sawdust 13
sensory processing disorder xi, xiii, 2, 3
sequins 15, 53
shampoo 13
shaving cream 8, 9, 11
sheets 38, 61
smell 1, 83
soap, dish. See detergent
songs 12, 43, 47, 53, 63
   Hammer Song 43
   Head and Shoulders 44
   Little Red Wagon 44
   London Bridge 58

Printed in the United States
138833LV00003B/1/A